How Genetics and Environment Shape Us:
The Destined Body

Obesity: Modern-Day Epidemic

How Genetics and Environment Shape Us:
The Destined Body

by
William Hunter

Mason Crest Publishers
Philadelphia

First printing
1 2 3 4 5 6 7 8 9 10

Library of Congress Cataloging-in-Publication Data

Hunter, William, 1971–
  How genetics and environment shape us : the destined body / by William Hunter.
     p. cm. — (Obesity : modern-day epidemic)
  Includes index.
  ISBN 1-59084-948-5—ISBN 1-59084-941-8 (series)
  1. Obesity—Genetic aspects—Juvenile literature. 2. Obesity—Social aspects—Juvenile literature. I. Title. II. Obesity (Philadelphia, Pa.)
  RC628.H865 2005
  616.3'98042—dc22
                                    2004027579

Produced by Harding House Publishing Service, Inc., Vestal, New York.
Cover design by Michelle Bouch.
Interior design by Michelle Bouch and MK Bassett-Harvey.
Printed in the Hashemite Kingdom of Jordan.

Contents

Introduction

We as a society often reserve our harshest criticism for those conditions we understand the least. Such is the case with obesity. Obesity is a chronic and often-fatal disease that accounts for 400,000 deaths each year. It is second only to smoking as a cause of premature death in the United States. People suffering from obesity need understanding, support, and medical assistance. Yet what they often receive is scorn.

Today, children are the fastest growing segment of the obese population in the United States. This constitutes a public health crisis of enormous proportions. Living with childhood obesity affects self-esteem, employment, and attainment of higher education. But childhood obesity is much more than a social stigma. It has serious health consequences.

Childhood obesity increases the risk for poor health in adulthood and premature death. Depression, diabetes, asthma, gallstones, orthopedic diseases, and other obesity-related conditions are all on the rise in children. Recent estimates suggest that 30 to 50 percent of children born in 2000 will develop type 2 diabetes mellitus—a leading cause of preventable blindness, kidney failure, heart disease, stroke, and amputations. Obesity is undoubtedly the most pressing nutritional disorder among young people today.

This series is an excellent first step toward understanding the obesity crisis and profiling approaches for remedying it. If we are to reverse obesity's current trend, there must be family, community, and national objectives promoting healthy eating and exercise. As a nation, we must demand broad-based public-health initiatives to limit TV watching, curtail junk food advertising toward children, and promote physical activity. More than rhetoric, these need to be our rallying cry. Anything short of this will eventually fail, and within our lifetime obesity will become the leading cause of death in the United States if not in the world.

Victor F. Garcia, M.D.
Founder, Bariatric Surgery Center
Cincinnati Children's Hospital Medical Center
Professor of Pediatrics and Surgery
School of Medicine
University of Cincinnati

Obesity:
A Growing Epidemic

If you ever watch the news, read a newspaper, or even scan the covers of magazines, you probably can't help but notice that people are always talking about health threats. In recent decades, an increasing focus on public health has led to many educational campaigns, often with impressive results. Smoking and alcohol use have decreased. There's greater public awareness about **AIDS** and how it can be prevented. Huge amounts of money and resources have been committed to treating (and hopefully one day curing) cancer and other diseases. But while the public has faced these obvious threats head-on, another health concern has been growing practically unnoticed. This new health threat has reached epidemic proportions. Obesity, the state of being very overweight, now threatens the health of millions of Americans.

Since 1980, obesity rates in the United States have doubled, going from 15 percent to nearly 30 percent of the adult population. As the number of people with obesity increases, the health complications and diseases associated with obesity also increase. Today, potentially deadly conditions like *coronary heart disease*, high blood pressure, *type 2 diabetes*, and many forms of cancer (all of which may be associated with or worsened by excess weight) are not only common among adults, they are also increasingly seen among children. In fact, some experts now believe that if the trend toward excess weight and obesity continues unchecked, this newest generation of young people may actually have a lower life expectancy than that of their parents! That's a serious claim, and it's causing more and more people to open their eyes to obesity and its health risks.

Despite increasing awareness of obesity as a serious health issue, many people continue to see obesity not as a legitimate medical condition but as a personal problem—a problem people bring on themselves through laziness, *gluttony*, or other destructive habits. Myths about obesity abound. People who are overweight or obese still face great *stigmatization* and discrimination in American society. Many people simply don't understand that one's weight isn't just a result of eating and exercise habits. Weight is also the product of *genetics* and complicated environmental factors, factors that are often outside a person's ability to control.

Defining Obesity

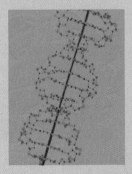

Clearly, excess weight and obesity are topics that deserve our attention. But before we can have a valuable discussion about obesity, where it comes from and how it can be prevented, we need to understand exactly what it is. If you look up the word *obesity* in the dictionary, you'll likely find a definition like this one: *a condition characterized by excessive body fat*. But how much does that tell you about what obesity really is? How does a person know if he has an appropriate or an excessive amount of fat? Most people think they can just step onto a bathroom scale, read a number, and know whether or not they have too much fat. Unfortunately, defining obesity is not nearly so simple. The human body is a complicated thing, and each body is unique. There is no magic number that can tell a person whether he is a healthy or unhealthy weight. In fact, weight isn't a very good measurement of obesity at all.

What Is Fat?

The technical term for fat is adipose tissue. Adipose tissue is made up of special cells that store lipids. Lipids are packed with energy; they contain more than twice as much energy per gram than carbohydrates or proteins. Adipose tissue, therefore, is the best way for the body to store excess energy. When you eat more food than you need to meet your daily energy requirements, your body converts the extra energy into lipids, which are stored as adipose tissue. This is not necessarily bad, because when you don't get enough energy, you burn that fat to keep you going. However, large quantities of adipose tissue can be dangerous. Most very healthy individuals have less than 15 percent body fat. In other words, at least 85 percent of their total body weight is made up of non-fat cells.

Why is weight a poor measure of obesity? Because different types of body tissues weigh different amounts. Muscle, for example, is a very dense, heavy tissue. Fat, however, is relatively light. In fact, muscle tissue is between eight and nine times heavier than an equal amount of fat tissue! A small amount of muscle, therefore, can be as heavy, or heavier, than a larger amount of fat.

Imagine two people. One weighs 150 pounds. The other weighs 140 pounds. Judging by weight alone, you might immediately assume that the

140-pound person is healthier and has less fat than the 150-pound person. If the 150-pound person, however, is very muscular, and the 140-pound person has practically no muscles at all, then your assumption would probably be wrong. The 140-pound person could actually be both lighter and "fatter" than the muscular 150-pound person. Instead of relying on weight alone to determine if someone is overweight or obese, doctors try to determine how much fat tissue the person has in comparison with lean tissue (muscles, bones, organs, and other healthy body tissues). This measurement is called percentage of body fat, and it is a much more accurate way of determining if someone is overweight or obese than weight alone.

Currently, the most common method for determining if someone is overweight or obese is with a formula called body mass index (BMI). The BMI formula is a calculation based on height and weight. The number the calculation yields is compared to ranges of numbers that correspond with medical definitions for "underweight," "normal," "overweight," or "obese." BMI can be calculated using one of the following formulas:

BMI = [weight in pounds ÷ (height in inches x height in inches)] x 703

or

BMI = weight in kilograms ÷ (height in meters x height in meters)

Here is an example for a person who is 5'3" tall (63") and weighs 120 pounds. The equation looks like this:

[120 ÷ (63 x 63)] x 703 = BMI
[120 ÷ (3969)] x 703 = BMI
[.03] x 703 = BMI
.03 x 703 = 21.09

The answer, in this case 21.09, is compared to the following chart.

BMI Classifications
According to the United States Centers for Disease Control and Prevention

BMI	CLASSIFICATION
< 18.5	= Underweight
18.5–24.9	= Normal
25.0–29.9	= Overweight
30.0 and above	= Obese

Research has shown that BMI calculations are usually a good indicator of the amount of body fat in most people. Furthermore, the calculation is easy. Just about anyone who knows her height and weight can calculate her BMI, even without the help of a physician. However, without a doctor's advice, a person shouldn't automatically assume that BMI is a completely accurate reflection of her health. Like judging by weight alone, BMI is not always accurate. For example, according to his BMI, the actor Brad Pitt is overweight. Few people looking at him would agree with this assessment. His "excess" weight is probably made up of muscles and lean tissue, not fat. So, even BMI is not a per-

More than 60 percent of all American adults are considered overweight or obese according to BMI calculations. Since 1996, a rapid rise in obesity rates among children has also been reported.

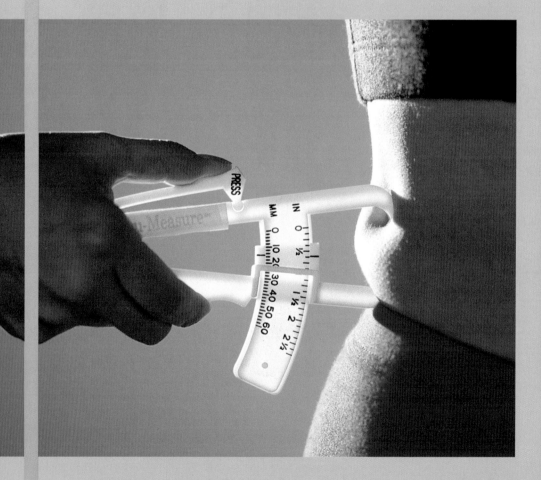

fect system. Typically, BMI overestimates the percentage of body fat in athletes and very muscular individuals. Many athletes would never even be considered overweight, yet by BMI calculations they could be classified as obese. BMI also often underestimates body fat in older individuals who are very light in weight. Typically, as we age our muscles atrophy, or break down, and are replaced by fatty tissues. Weight decreases as more and more muscle is replaced with fat. Since BMI is a ratio of weight to height, a decrease in weight decreases the BMI score even though in truth the percentage of body fat is increasing, and so is the health risk.

Since BMI is not always an accurate indicator of an individual's amount of body fat, health-care professionals may employ other means for measuring body fat percentage. One common method is to use skin-fold measurements in various areas of the body where fat tends to collect. Special tools called calipers are used to pinch the skin in common "trouble areas" such as beneath the arm and on the stomach. These measurements tell how much fat is just beneath the surface of the skin (this is called subcutaneous fat). Most often seven folds are measured, and the results are averaged to produce a relatively accurate assessment of the percentage of fat throughout the body.

Several problems can affect the readings of skin-fold calipers. The skin-fold method can be difficult to master, resulting in inaccurate readings. Also, deep deposits of fat, such as those that surround the internal organs, may grow faster than the subcutaneous fat. These deep deposits, however, can't be measured with calipers, so one's body fat percentage may be higher than the caliper measurements suggest. The body fat percentage of obese individuals may also be underestimated by the skin-fold method because their skin may be stretched, less elastic, and therefore less "pinchable." Measuring with calipers is still one of the most common ways of determining body fat percentage, but like BMI, it can be inaccurate for some people.

Bioelectrical impedance analysis (BIA) is another way the amount of body fat can be determined. In BIA, a small electrical current is run from one elec-

trode through the body to another electrode, and the result interpreted by a computer. Electricity passes through lean tissue more easily than through fat tissue. A person whose body contains a greater amount of fat, therefore, will have more resistance to the electrical current than a person whose body contains less fat. The computer uses the amount of resistance to estimate the amount of fat in the person's body.

The BIA method is quick and easy. Most people need little or no training to operate a BIA scale. In fact, such scales are available at most local drugstores. All a person needs to use one is a place to set it down (BIA scales are usually about the same size as a regular bathroom scale) and an electrical outlet or a good battery. But, as we've seen so far, no method for determining body fat appears to be perfect, and BIA is no exception. Many doctors feel that BIA scales are too inaccurate and frown on their use. The manufacturers advise that users rid their bodies of as much urine as possible before taking a reading because bodily fluids can affect the results. A large amount of fluid will reduce the resistance, causing a lowered reading. At times, the altered reading will be as much as ten percent off from the true value. BIA, even when used correctly, tends to overestimate the percentage of body fat for lean people and to underestimate it for obese people.

> *According to the National Institutes of Health, overweight and obesity are the second leading cause of preventable death in the United States each year.*

Because there is no perfectly accurate way to estimate a person's percentage of body fat, doctors usually combine such measurements with other indicators of health. One of the most common ways that doctors measure a person's risk for developing obesity-related health problems is by measuring waist circumference (how big around a person's waist is). Typically, men whose waists measure greater than forty inches and women whose waists measure thirty-five inches or greater are considered at higher risk for obesity-related health problems. Generally, no single method for determining obesity should be relied on to give an accurate picture of the health of an individual. Combining two or more of the more common techniques reduces the risk of errors and provides much more accurate information for the doctor.

The Costs of Obesity

Being overweight or obese can have great costs to your health. The greater a person's amount of excess weight, the greater his chance of health problems like heart disease, heart attack, stroke, high blood pressure, type 2 diabetes, various cancers, reproductive complications, *osteoarthritis*, and more. Excess weight can also affect one's quality of life by reducing mobility, decreasing energy, and exposing the individual to hurtful social stigma. These are all serious costs for the individual. There are also serious costs for society as a whole.

Obesity affects every country in the world. As the number of obese people who need medical attention as a result of their condition increases, the costs begin to add up. According to the National Institutes of Health (NIH), worldwide costs of the surge in obesity since 1970 are estimated to be in excess of $800 billion each year and rising. The costs of health insurance, drugs, and treatments are being driven up as more and more people are forced to use the medical system to treat the various health problems associated with obesity.

Currently, no country in the world is as affected by the obesity crisis as much as the United States. The NIH reports that, in the United States, the financial costs associated with obesity rose to more than $117 billion in 2002. The direct costs, those that come from preventing, diagnosing, and treating the condition, accounted for about $61 billion of the total. The

remaining dollars are the estimated wages lost from workers who are absent due to obesity-related illness, disability, or death.

Health-care costs and lost wages are not the only ways that obesity digs into our wallets. Americans also spend a huge amount of money trying to lose weight. An entire industry has sprung up offering weight-control treatments and services. Americans spend more than $33 billion a year on over-the-counter remedies, many of which are not proven effective or safe. An increase in sales of various diet programs, such as the Atkins® Diet or the South Beach Diet®, led to a rapid change in the way people try to lose weight in recent years. People are desperate to control their weight and often embarrassed to see a doctor for help. Thus, they turn to often-expensive and usually ineffective diets, programs, and "miracle" cures that may dent the pocketbook but do little to improve health.

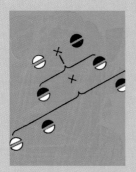

Why Do We Gain or Lose Weight?

Whether a person gains, maintains, or loses weight is based on something called energy balance. Maintaining a healthy body mass relies on balancing the amount of energy taken in with the amount of energy used over a period of time. An increase in energy intake without a similar increase in physical activity results in an increase in body fat. A decrease in energy intake without a decrease in physical activity results in a decrease in body fat. For most of human history, it seems that striking a balance between energy intake and energy output wasn't difficult for the majority of humans. Life was hard and required a great deal of physical activity, so all the energy taken in was almost guaranteed to be burned. But our lifestyles have changed a lot in recent years, and keeping things in balance has become harder. Obesity has increased as a result.

In countries like the United States, life has definitely gotten easier for

Calories: The Measurement of Food Energy

Energy in food is measured using a unit called a Calorie. A Calorie is a measurement of heat. Calorie with a capital "C" stands for large calorie or kilocalorie. It is the amount of energy it takes to raise one kilogram (approximately one liter or 4.25 cups) of water by one degree Celsius. There is also a calorie with a small "c." This unit is equal to the amount of energy it takes to heat one gram of water (or about twenty drops from an eye dropper) by one degree Celsius. There are 1,000 calories in one Calorie.

most people—at least in the sense that starvation is not knocking at the door. Few people have to perform physical labor from sunup to sundown to guarantee there's food on the table. (Those who do rarely suffer from obesity.) More people than ever work at jobs that may give the mind a workout, but leave the body *sedentary*. In addition, our entertainment and favorite pastimes involve less physical activity than ever before. For many people, televisions and computers have completely replaced sports and physical activities. Then, on top of it all, Americans today have access to greater amounts of more Calorie-rich foods than ever before. Add these factors together, and you can easily upset energy balance, resulting in excess weight.

These changes in lifestyle and habits are often cited as the cause of America's obesity epidemic, but we can't overlook other important factors. Genetics and environment also have a strong effect on a person's weight. Today, genetic and environmental factors are working together with lifestyle changes in interesting ways to affect Americans' weight and health.

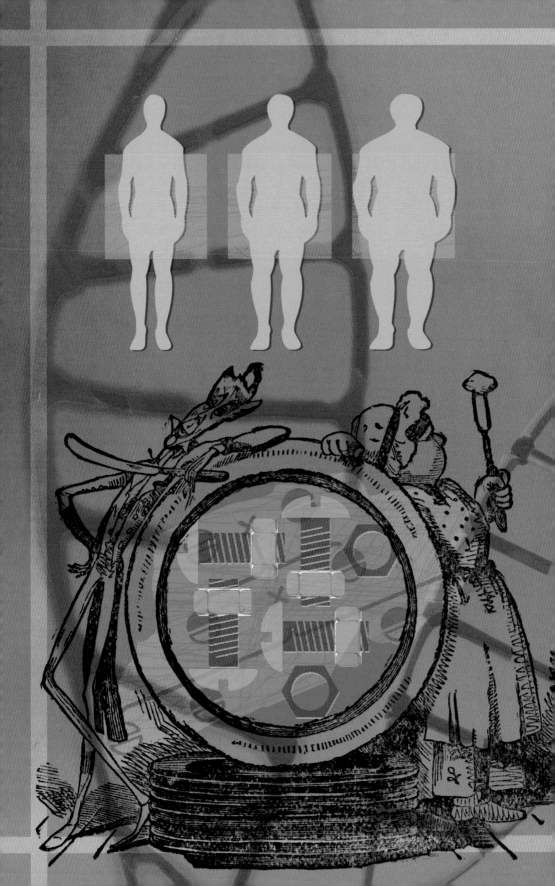

Chapter 2

The Nuts and Bolts of Genetics

- A Brief History of Genetics

- The Scientific Basis of Genetics

A Brief History of Genetics

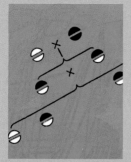

Since the beginning of recorded time people understood that there was some connection between parents and their offspring. People didn't necessarily understand exactly why some characteristics were carried on through generations, but they could certainly see evidence that this was so. In fact, early on, people realized that heredity, the carrying on of characteristics from one generation to the next, could be very useful. Archaeological evidence indicates that ancient civilizations used *selective breeding* to develop crops that produced better and animals that were larger, calmer, and more suitable for controlling in herds than the typical plants and animals in the wild. The ancient Egyptians even kept written records of their methods for improving crops and herds. Despite a *rudimentary* understanding that heredity existed and could be manipulated, however, people did not begin to understand the actual biological mechanisms at work until quite recently. In the nineteenth century, an Austrian *monk* by the name of Gregor Mendel went to work exploring the passing of character traits from generation to generation, and the field of genetics was born.

Mendel spent most of his early years teaching mathematics, physics, and Greek at his *monastery* and dabbling in basic genetics experiments. Several small discoveries led to the development of a much larger experiment in which Mendel studied how character traits in plants pass from one generation to the next. Mendel chose to study pea plants because he could examine two generations each year. Thirty-eight thousand plants later, Mendel had gathered the information that became the basis for all future genetics research.

Mendel's research clearly showed that some parental characteristics passed to the next generation. Furthermore, the traits could be separated from each other by selective breeding. In other words, not all of the charac-

teristics from the parents'
generation would express them-
selves in the offspring. Exactly which characteristics were
expressed depended on which plants were paired for breeding.
Take the characteristic of height. The parent plant's height
would not always be expressed in the offspring. For example,
when a short plant was bred with a tall plant, all the offspring plants were
tall; the "shortness" characteristic from the one parent was not expressed in
the offspring.

Mendel theorized that the plants must have individual information units
that carried the information for each physical characteristic. In the case of
height, the information unit for "tallness" had to be dominating or canceling
out the information unit for "shortness." He called these information units
genes and theorized that some genes were dominant and others recessive.
Whichever characteristic expressed itself would be the dominant gene.

Genetics has come a long way since Mendel's time. Today, many of his
experiments and assumptions seem like common knowledge, but they were
great discoveries that allowed scientists to begin cracking the code of heredity. Today, progress in the field of genetics has taught us that many traits,
including a person's likelihood of developing certain diseases, are determined before that person is born.

The Scientific Basis of Genetics

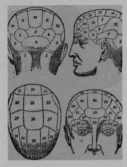

To understand how physical traits are determined, we must understand the basic way information is passed from one generation to the next. All the information for your body is stored in something called deoxyribonucleic acid—DNA. Each cell in a person's body contains a complete copy of the DNA inherited from each parent. The DNA is made up of genes, which are organized into long strands called chromosomes. Human beings have forty-six chromosomes arranged into twenty-three pairs. Half the chromosomes come from one's mother. The other half come from one's father.

An individual's chromosomal pairs are formed at the moment of conception—when the sperm cell and the egg cell unite. Unlike other cells in the body, the sex cells (sperm cells and eggs cells) do not have pairs of chromosomes. Rather, they contain only twenty-three single chromosomes, or one-half the amount of other cells. When the sperm cell and egg cell meet, their

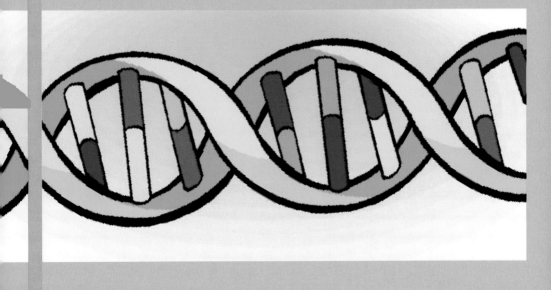

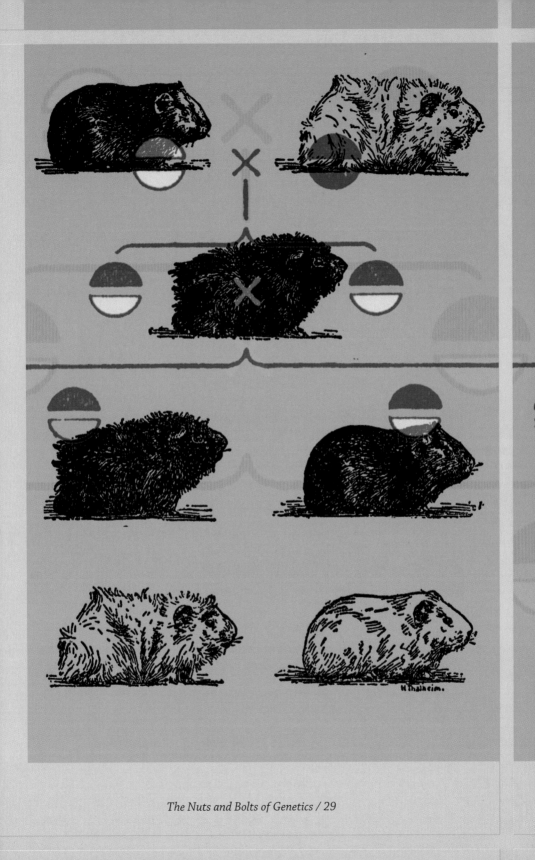

By the 1950s, scientists knew that genetic information was carried from person to person through DNA. No one, however, knew what DNA looked like or how it replicated itself. In the early 1950s, British scientist Rosalind Franklin concentrated on studying DNA. It was her work that led to the April 25, 1953, *Nature* article by Dr. James Watson and Professor Francis Crick that finally unveiled DNA's structure. Using her research as the base, they discovered the double helix, or corkscrew-like, structure of DNA. They showed that when cells divide, the two strands that make up the helix separate. Each strand becomes the base for a new helix. With rare exceptions, an exact copy of the DNA results from the "unzipping" and replication of the first strand. Watson and Crick's work was practically ignored for seven years, but eventually, its importance was recognized. The discovery of the DNA structure has been called the most important scientific discovery of the last one hundred years.

twenty-three individual chromosomes unite to form the twenty-three pairs. The cell, with its complete set of DNA, will copy itself over and over again until a whole new human being is formed, with traits from both of her parents.

All genes work basically the same way: they cause the production of specific proteins that control the appearance of the trait in question. The tech-

nical term for the production of specific proteins is expression. The characteristics a person has depends on which genes are expressed, and the person may have different forms of genes for a single characteristic.

Each form of a gene is called an allele. Different alleles of a gene will cause the expression of different proteins, resulting in a different appearance. To use Mendel's plant experiment again, Mendel discovered that there was a gene for height. The gene for "tallness" was one form, or allele, of the height gene, while the gene for "shortness" was another form, or allele, of the height gene. An example for humans is eye color—there are several alleles of the genes that control eye color.

The Human Genome Project: Unlocking the DNA Mystery and Creating Controversy

In October 1990, the U.S. Department of Energy and the National Institutes of Health formed the Human Genome Project to "map" human DNA. The project's goals included identifying 20,000 to 25,000 genes in human DNA, determining the sequences of the chemical base pairs, establishing an information database where all the project's discoveries could be stored, and transferring the technology to the private sector. The Human Genome Project became a worldwide effort and was completed in 2003. Now analysis of the data has begun.

Not everyone, however, supports the Human Genome Project. In fact, it's quite controversial. The project has discovered which genes are responsible for some diseases, birth defects, and debilitating adulthood conditions. On the one hand, knowing that a person has the genetic potential to develop a certain disease could have health benefits like allowing doctors to formulate prevention and treatment plans for that person before the disease gets expressed. However, there are also ethical and social issues that come with knowing someone has the genetic potential for a disease. For example, should insurance companies have access to people's genetic information and therefore be able to deny coverage to affected individuals; what is the psychological impact of knowing you will or have a great potential to develop a certain disease; and to what extent should knowledge of a fetus's genetic code be taken into account when determining whether or not a pregnancy should be carried to term?

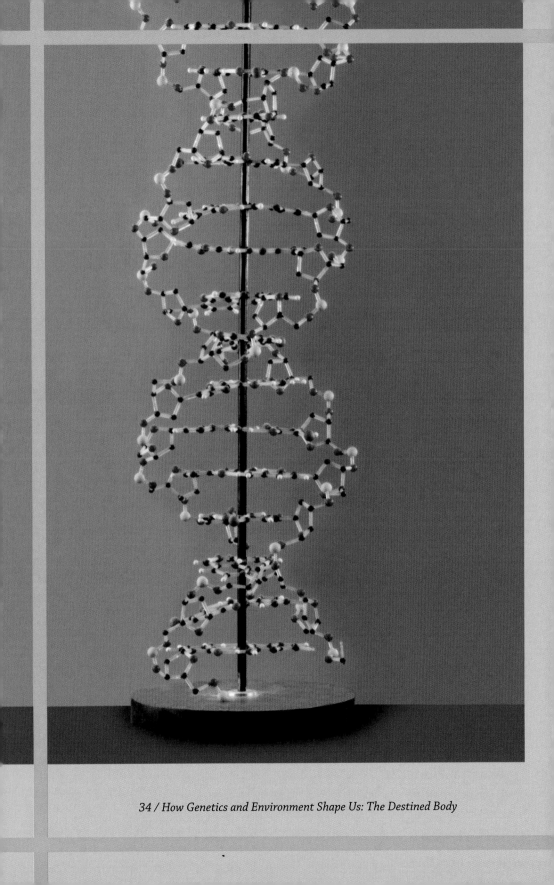

Mendel discovered that some alleles (like the "tallness" allele) were dominant and other alleles (like the "shortness" allele) were recessive in plants. The same is true for people. Think about eye color again. A person who inherits an allele for brown eyes from one parent and an allele for blue eyes from the other parent will have brown eyes because that is the dominant allele. The recessive alleles, however, do not simply disappear. They still exist in the genetic code; they just aren't being physically expressed. Since they still exist, they can be passed to offspring even though they are not necessarily identifiable in the parent.

Alleles are always inherited in pairs. One allele comes from each parent. A person who inherits two of the same alleles is called homozygous for that particular allele. A person who inherits two different alleles is called heterozygous. In the case of homozygous alleles, the dominance of the allele does not matter because both alleles are the same. People who are heterozygous will have two different alleles for a trait and will display whichever allele is dominant.

Advances in genetic research have helped us understand that Mendel's explanations, while essentially correct, were overly simplistic in assuming that each trait was controlled by just one set of alleles. Scientists have discovered that sometimes more than one gene can have an effect on a trait. Many traits, such as eye color, are controlled by three or more genes. Eye color is therefore called a polygenic (or many genes) trait. Many traits in humans are determined by more than one gene. Each allele may only have a very small effect on the overall development of the trait, but when combined with the other genes can have a very strong effect on the appearance of the individual. Again, eye color is a good example. Eye color is not controlled by just one gene or all people would have either brown eyes (from inheriting the dominant brown allele) or blue eyes (from inheriting two recessive blue alleles). But try to identify all the shades of eye color in your family. You will notice that not everyone has exactly the same eye color. Polygenic traits are usually neither fully dominant nor fully recessive. The effect of these genes relies on the combination. Polygenic traits are a blend of all the genes affecting them.

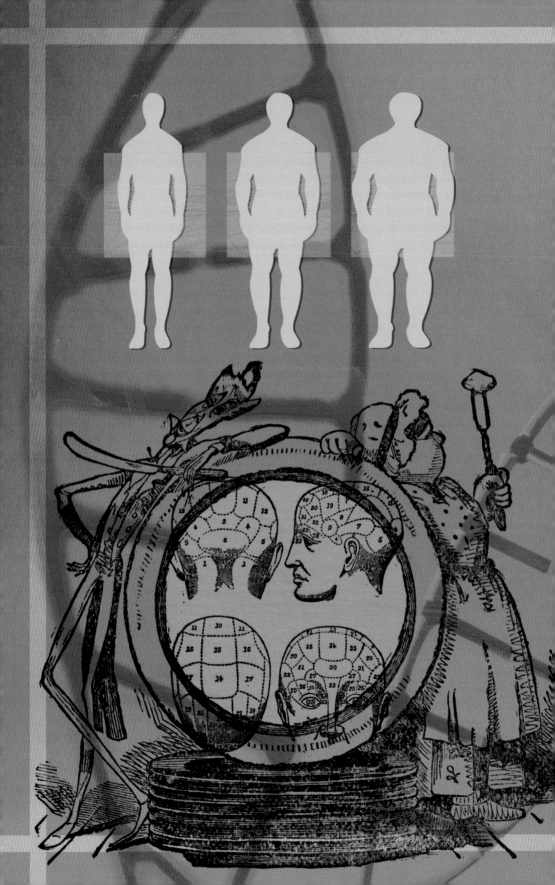

Chapter 3

The Genetics of Obesity

- Single-Gene Disorders Causing Obesity
- Polygenic Causes of Obesity
- Evolution Gone Awry?

Today we understand that the information stored in our DNA determines not only simple things like our hair and eye color, but all kinds of things about our bodies. DNA appears to determine a person's *susceptibility* to certain diseases. It may also play a role in the development of certain behaviors. Much of the research and theories concerning DNA's role in these complicated issues of mind and body is controversial. One thing, however, is for sure; there is greater evidence than ever before that our physical traits are inherited.

Advances in genetics have opened many doors over the past few years. Scientists have explored using genetic therapies for many illnesses, such as Parkinson's disease and Alzheimer's disease. Genetic counseling can be used to screen prospective parents to determine the risk of inherited diseases like Huntington's disease before conceiving a child. In some cases, genes have been found to be a relatively good predictor of future health. But what about with obesity? Many people do not think of obesity as a *chronic* medical condition worthy of treatment. However, today most scientists and medical professionals are drawing the conclusion that obesity is a disease. Yes, simple excess weight can result from poor eating and lifestyle habits. But obesity is a serious condition that rarely results from simply making bad eating and exercise choices. Obese individuals almost always have some genetic *predisposition* to the disease, and science is uncovering the factors that come into play in the development of obesity.

In the years since Mendel's research, techniques for studying the effects of particular genes have been developed. Human DNA has about three billion individual pieces. The genes themselves are only three individual pieces long, meaning that there could be one billion genes in each person's genetic makeup. Thankfully, much of our DNA is not made up of genes, but of pieces that, at present, scientists believe do not control anything. Most researchers agree that people have between twenty-five and thirty thousand genes. Although science is working to map and identify each of these, it is a long, complex process. Scientists are now able to identify the genes that cause some specific health problems, but there is still much work to be done.

Understanding and locating genes can be a long process because there are so many genes to screen and because multiple genes often control a particular trait. These polygenic conditions are very difficult to study and require much more work than do traits controlled by only one gene. It can take many years to successfully isolate the causes of a polygenic condition.

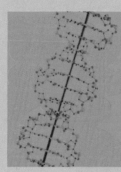

Single-Gene Disorders Causing Obesity

The genetic disorders that are easiest for scientists to identify are single-gene disorders. In single-gene disorders, only one gene is involved in creating the condition. In the case of obesity, a few conditions have

The DNA sequence of the human genome contains so much information that if it were compiled in books, 200 volumes the size of a Manhattan telephone book (1,000 pages each) would be needed to hold it all. It would take about 9.5 years to read out loud (without stopping) the 3 billion bases in the genome sequence. This is calculated on a reading rate of 10 bases per second, equaling 600 bases per minute, 36,000 bases per hour, 864,000 bases per day, and 315,360,000 bases per year.

been found where a single mutated, or changed, gene has led to severe obesity. One of these conditions involves a mutation to the gene responsible for the production of a protein called leptin.

Leptin is a protein that is very important in controlling the amount of food we eat and the amount of energy we expend. Fatty tissue produces leptin, so as the levels of fat in our bodies increase, so do the levels of leptin. Special receptors, or sensors, in the brain can sense the amount of leptin in the bloodstream. If those receptors recognize a large amount of leptin in your blood, they will tell your body to make you feel less hungry. If they detect less leptin, they will tell your body to make you feel hungrier. However, the receptors only recognize normal leptin, so a slight mutation to that protein can short-circuit the whole system. In people who have this genetic mutation, the receptors do not recognize the leptin in the body, so they never tell the body to suppress or turn off its hunger. For people with this condition, the results can be horrible: constant, insatiable hunger that often leads to excessive eating and uncontrollable weight gain. It is very difficult to ignore hunger, as anyone who has ever been on a diet can tell you!

Changes in leptin can have an effect on many other important processes in a person's body as well. Leptin is important in the production of red blood cells, wound healing, and immune system responses. In addition, mutations to the gene that produces leptin greatly increase the risk of a person developing type 2 diabetes. Insulin, the hormone that allows sugar to pass into cells where it is burned for energy, depends on leptin to regulate its production.

Patients who have this genetic mutation have shown promising results with leptin-replacement therapies. Studies have shown that replacing leptin can be very successful in reducing weight to healthier levels. One study of leptin replacement reported that several patients whose average BMI was 52 or above lost enough weight in the course of one year to reduce their average BMI to a more healthy 29. This represents a massive weight loss and a great treatment success for this particular disorder.

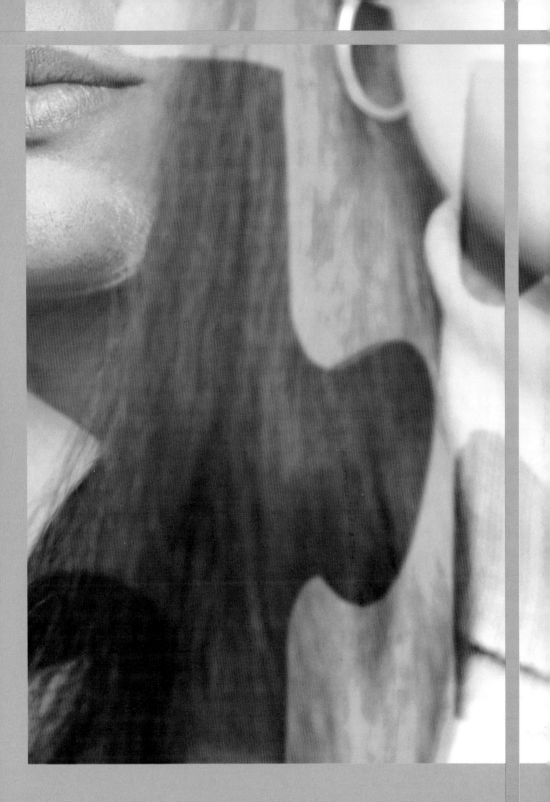

> *Only about 3 percent of the total genome is composed of genes. The remaining 97 percent is often referred to as "junk DNA." This, however, is not a good name. Much of the "junk" has some function; we just haven't yet discovered what that function is.*

Leptin, however, is not the only factor in regulating appetite. In fact, appetite is a complicated bodily function, and many factors influence it. Perhaps the most common single-gene condition that causes obesity is one that results in a small mutation of a receptor for an appetite-regulating hormone called melanocortin. Melanocortin requires a specific protein in the brain to function properly. A modification of that one protein can lead to severe obesity beginning early in childhood. Much like in the case of people whose bodies do not recognize leptin, the individual just cannot control his hunger and will eat more than is necessary at every meal. The excess energy is converted into fat, and the person gains weight.

Another single-gene disorder that carries a greatly increased risk of obesity is Bardet-Biedl Syndrome (BBS). One of the most common symptoms of BBS is early-onset obesity. Patients with BBS are unable to control their hunger and will eat far more than is necessary at every sitting. In addition,

the other symptoms of BBS can make it very difficult for the individual to use excess calories properly, furthering the tendency to gain weight. Prader-Willi Syndrome (PWS) is another disorder that can cause obesity. One in every twelve thousand children is diagnosed with this disease every year. The symptoms of PWS include uncontrolled appetite and extreme overeating, even in infants. Children with PWS are usually obsessed with food and eating, mainly because their body systems are not functioning properly.

Research into single-gene disorders that cause obesity is ongoing with new discoveries made all the time. However, in many health conditions, one single factor is rarely to blame, and obesity is no exception. In fact, obesity caused by single-gene conditions is exceptional. Even if a person's obesity is genetic in nature, the chances are her condition is caused by multiple factors and multiple genes. In such a case, a person's obesity would have polygenic causes.

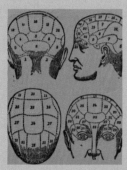

Polygenic Causes of Obesity

Most people who have a genetic tendency to be overweight have this tendency because of much more complex causes. In fact, most researchers agree that between three and six genes are responsible for increased risk of obesity. A slight mutation to any one of these genes will not likely have a large effect on a person. Similarly, having one or two of the genes thought to be warning signs for increased risk of obesity will not usually cause problems. But the more of these obesity-related genes that are affected, the greater one's risk of developing obesity will be. Polygenic conditions are often thought to add up; the effects are not felt until a number of genes work together to create the effect.

A number of genes believed to be key contributors in the development of polygenic obesity have been identified. Interestingly, most of the genes were

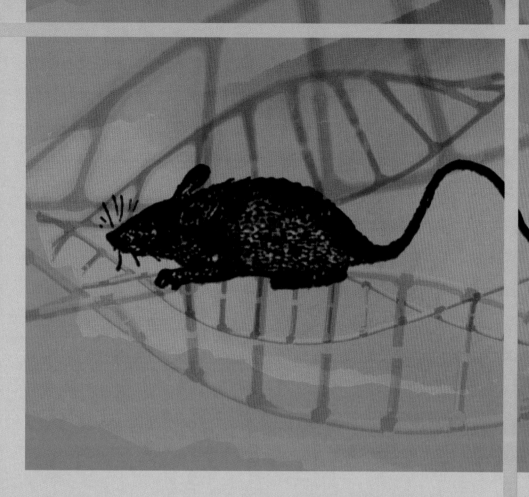

found by using mice. It turns out mice and humans share many genes. A mutation to a gene called UCP, now known to cause the production of a protein that is very important in the way our bodies use energy, can prevent us from burning calories efficiently. Mutations to another gene, called NOB1, can cause a huge increase in the amount of insulin in a person's bloodstream, which can also lead to obesity. Scientists recently discovered that the gene GAD2 is needed for the production of neuropeptide-Y, a hormone needed to control hunger.

Most often, genes thought to be involved in the development of obesity are in some way related to our hunger-control systems. Obviously, if we don't stop eating when full, we are going to gain weight (unless we balance the increased eating with an equal increase in exercise). In addition, some scientists have begun to look at how our bodies burn energy. They theorize that mutations to genes that affect the way we use energy would also play a role in obesity. It seems likely that changes in the way a person's body uses energy would also lead to changes in weight. Realizing that obesity has genetic components has helped us learn a great deal about how some processes in our bodies work. Scientists have even learned about how fat is stored and controlled in the body by studying the genetic conditions that increase the risk of obesity.

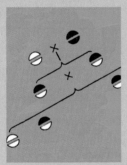

Evolution Gone Awry?

Most of the genetic factors involved in obesity that we have looked at have to do with a person's ability to control hunger. Many scientists, however, believe that the ability to eat despite not being hungry may be just as much a genetic trait as the hunger mechanisms themselves. After all, a person can eat even when he is not hungry. Feeling hungry all the time would certainly encourage a person to eat, but let's face it, few people eat only when hungry. People eat for many reasons: because we're happy, sad, bored, visiting with family or friends, or just because something tastes good. We can "eat through a full feeling," so to speak. So hunger alone, or the genetic biological mechanisms that control hunger, may not be solely to blame when a person begins to gain weight.

Throughout much of human history, the ability to eat even when one wasn't hungry was necessary for survival. In those days, food was scarce. It was important to eat as much as possible while food was available because there was no guarantee that there would be more food the next day. It was better to eat too much and have the extra energy stored as fat than to eat too little and starve to death. Therefore, many scientists theorize, our hunger

mechanism and ability to eat despite lack of hunger have evolved to be stronger than our hunger-control mechanism.

In today's world, our evolution is working against us. Obviously, food is not nearly so hard to come by nowadays, and periods with little food are quite rare in the United States. However, it takes a very long time for evolution to remove a trait, and modern humans are still more likely to have a malfunction in their ability to stop eating than in their ability to ignore hunger. It is now more dangerous to eat too much in times of plenty (which are almost all the time for modern Americans) than it is to ignore hunger and risk times without food.

Genetics, however, remains an extremely complicated topic. Even when genetic links to obesity are found, the existence of these links does not mean the genetic factors can be positively identified as the cause of a person's obesity. It is very difficult to separate the effect of environment from the effect of genetics. Some scientists believe that environmental factors are at least as influential as genetic factors in America's rising obesity rates.

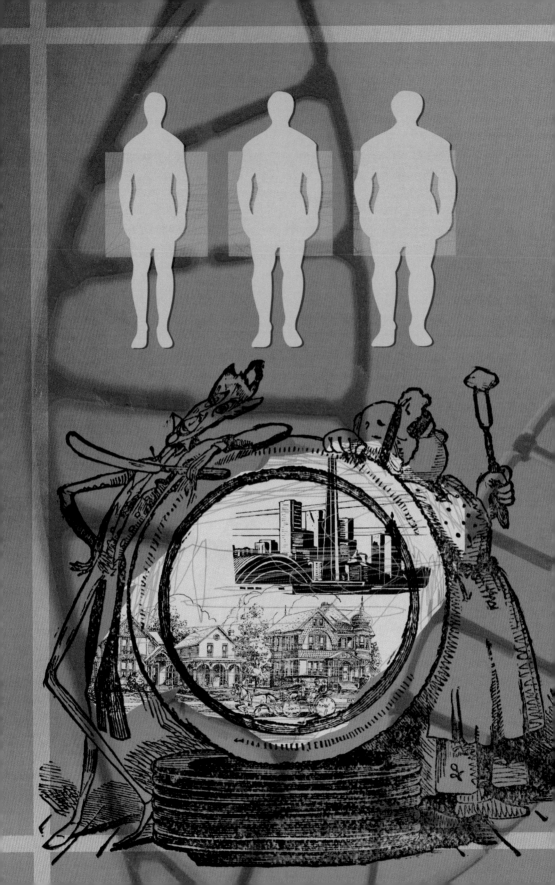

Chapter 4

Environmental Factors and Obesity

- What Is an Environmental Factor?

- Environmental Factors That Increase Energy Intake

- Environmental Factors That Decrease Physical Activity

- Behavior: An Environmental Factor?

What Is an Environmental Factor?

Many scientists, *sociologists*, and other researchers believe that environment plays a much larger role in the development of obesity than genetics. After all, if genetics were solely to blame, why a sudden increase in obesity now? Why wouldn't humans have suffered from obesity throughout history? Have our genes suddenly gone berserk, mutating right and left in just the last thirty years? Or is another factor at work? Evidence suggests that at least some external factors are to blame. According to recent studies, since 1970, people have slowly but steadily reduced their physical activity while increasing their energy intake. Research has shown that a steady annual increase in the average weight of United States citizens has been building up over the years. The average American gains forty pounds between the ages of twenty and forty.

Environmental factors are sometimes difficult to identify. They are the things around us—the conditions, circumstances, and influences in our environment—that affect the way grow, live, and behave. Environmental factors can include things like where you live, what activities are available to

In 2001 the U.S. Surgeon General recommended that all restaurants provide detailed nutrition information about their foods so that people can make informed choices.

you, and what foods are common in your home. Environmental factors exist both on a small and large scale. Small-scale environmental factors would be those that you are exposed to through your immediate everyday contacts with your family and friends. Large-scale environmental factors are conditions taking place on a larger scale, like things happening in your state, in the country, or in the world.

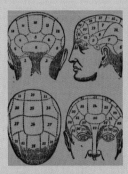

Environmental Factors That Increase Energy Intake

One environmental factor that is likely impacting obesity rates is an overall change in American eating habits. Basically, Americans are eating more than they've ever eaten before. This trend is most easily visible in restaurants. Restaurants across the country have gradually increased the size of the portions they serve. One reason for this increase may be our value system: when making purchases, most Americans would agree that it's important to get "more for your money." Most Americans are just as likely to apply this concept to food as to any other product or service. Restaurants are not about to sit back and ignore this. They realize that they will lose business if their customers can get more food for the same amount of money elsewhere. Most portion sizes have increased as much as 40 percent since 1970. Everything from the appetizers, to the main courses, to the soft drinks has gotten larger. For example, years ago a large soda was approximately twelve ounces. Now, twenty ounces or more is not uncommon, and this often comes with unlimited free refills.

A study published by the *Journal of the American Medical Association* examined the American trend toward larger portion sizes and confirmed that between the years 1971 and 1999, portion sizes for certain foods increased

dramatically. Of the foods studied—hamburgers, Mexican food, soft drinks, snacks, and pizza—all but pizza increased. Hamburgers became, on average, more than a fifth larger. A plate of Mexican food was more than one-quarter larger. Soft drinks had expanded by more than half their previous size, and salty snacks like potato chips, pretzels, and crackers had grown by 60 percent. Perhaps even more disturbing, the study showed that portion sizes aren't just increasing in restaurants; they are also increasing at home. Whether eating out or eating in, Americans in general are eating more.

Is it fair, however, to say that increased portion sizes play a role in rising obesity rates? After all, just because a person gives you more food doesn't mean you have to eat more, right? Well, maybe you don't have to eat more,

When McDonald's, perhaps the most famous of the fast-food restaurants, opened its doors for the first time it didn't even have medium and large options. Fries were fries, and they came in what today would look like a very small package. Today, however, slogans like "Get more for your money!" and "Bigger is better!" are fast-food mantras. Practically every fast-food restaurant has its own version of the "value meal." Wendy's has Biggie® drinks, Biggie® fries, and if those aren't big enough, a Great Biggie® size. Burger King has King drinks and King fries, and until recently McDonald's had the famous Supersize®. In some restaurants, what was once a regular-size fries or drink is now the "kiddie size," and what used to be a large is now a small.

but chances are you will eat more. This may be where those millennia of trying to ward off starvation come in. Studies have shown that the average person eats more when faced with a large portion of food than when faced with a small portion of food (even if he doesn't finish either portion).

Recently, researchers at Penn State University's College of Health and Human Development studied this "overeating" phenomenon. In their study, they gave volunteers two differently sized portions of macaroni and cheese and told them to eat until they were full. The results astounded the researchers. When the volunteers were given the smaller portion size, they stopped eating sooner, even if they didn't clean their plates. When given the larger portion size, the volunteers ate an average of 30 percent more (again even if they didn't clean their plates). But perhaps most surprising of all, the volunteers did not report feeling fuller after eating more. The volunteers did

The Glycemic Index:
A New Way of Judging Carbohydrates

According to the Harvard School of Public Health, the carbohydrate story may be even more complicated than separating carbs into "simple" and "complex." Generally, simple carbohydrates are considered bad because they trigger a quick rise in blood-sugar levels. As Harvard researchers point out, however, not all simple carbohydrates actually cause such a rise. Many types of fruit, for example, contain simple carbohydrates but are also high in fiber and are digested more slowly. Similarly, a high-fat food containing simple carbohydrates (like ice cream) will also be broken down more slowly, resulting in a gradual rise rather than a spike in blood sugar. The Harvard School of Public Health suggests that people judge carbohydrates not in terms of simple or complex, but according to something called the Glycemic Index. The Glycemic Index rates foods by their effect on blood sugar. High-glycemic foods (like potatoes and white bread) make blood-sugar levels spike. Low-glycemic foods (like most legumes, whole fruits, and whole wheat) make blood-sugar levels rise gradually.

not realize they had eaten more at the large-portion sittings, and in fact, most didn't even notice the portion size had increased! Eating 30 percent more at every sitting could very easily cause energy imbalance and quickly lead to weight gain.

The American diet, however, hasn't only changed regarding the amount of food we eat. It's also changed in the types of food we eat. High-fat foods have long been a popular part of our diets. Fatty foods contain much more energy than other food types (remember the discussion of fat we had in chapter 1?). Most dietary research suggests that people should limit the daily amount of fatty foods they consume to less than 30 percent of their total energy intake. Despite these recommendations, the average person consistently consumes between 35 and 40 percent of her daily energy from fat. Increasing fat intake is an easy way to increase energy consumption and create an energy imbalance.

Fatty foods, on the one hand, are very high in energy (or Calories) and will therefore cause weight gain if consumed in excessive quantities. On the other hand, fatty foods tend to be heavy, harder for your body to break down, and therefore quite filling. Some people suggest that fatty foods aren't the problem for most people because fatty foods are filling and consumed in smaller amounts than other foods.

Today, much attention has turned away from fatty foods and focused on carbohydrates. According to new theories, the foods people really have to watch out for if they don't want to gain weight are foods high in sugar and easy for the body to break down. These include white rice, white bread, non-whole-wheat pasta, candy, and other simple carbohydrates. Unlike complex carbohydrates (like whole grains and high-fiber foods), simple carbohydrates are very easy for the body to break down into a simple sugar called glucose. These foods yield so much glucose so quickly that usually the body can't use it all at once. The body has to convert that glucose to fat and store it for later. Even if some of this food gets stored as fat, you may soon feel hungry again because the digestion process happened so quickly. For these reasons, some people theorize that these high-sugar foods actually play a bigger role in America's obesity crisis than do high-fat foods. Either way, with a huge increase in Americans' reliance on fast foods and prepackaged meals and snacks, both high-fat and high-sugar foods now make up a large part of the average diet.

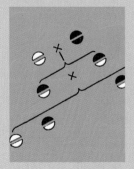

Environmental Factors That Decrease Physical Activity

The amount of food you take in isn't the only factor in energy balance. The other side of the scale is physical activity. The fact that Americans are eating more

A report from the National Academies' Institute of Medicine says that people who succeed in maintaining a healthy weight tend to get at least one hour of moderate-intensity physical activity daily (one example is walking at 4 miles per hour for a total of 60 minutes).

wouldn't necessarily be a problem at all if they were also performing more physical activity to balance out the scale. Unfortunately, Americans aren't increasing their physical activity. In fact, the average amount of physical activity performed by Americans has decreased over the years. A number of environmental factors are thought to be to blame.

One reason our physical activity has decreased is because of changes in the types of work we do. Let's look, for example, at jobs in the manufacturing sector. Manufacturing used to involve a lot of physical labor because people were actually making things with their own hands. Machines and computers, however, have done a lot to change this. Today, many people working in manufacturing aren't actually making anything with their own hands. They are operating computerized machinery. Often, all an operator must do is pull a lever or press a button. Robotic technology has greatly reduced the physical effort of manufacturing. Most employees are now required to do very little lifting or other highly physical labor at work.

Just as important as *mechanization* in manufacturing is a growth in professional employment. Today, more and more jobs require people to put their minds to use but leave their bodies at home (so to speak). Many Americans now hold positions in fields that require little or no moving about

Gym Class

According to the United States Centers for Disease Control and Prevention, only six to eight percent of senior, middle, and elementary schools provide daily physical education for the entire school year for all students. Only 65 percent of high school students participate in vigorous physical activity three or more days a week, and only 27 percent participate in moderate physical activity five or more days a week. Furthermore, about 93 percent of high schools operate vending machines, school stores, or snack bars, but only 21 percent of schools sell low-fat yogurt or fruits and vegetables in these venues.

during the day. For the most part, all the person's body needs to do is sit at a desk and perhaps occasionally fetch a file or walk to a meeting. The growth of employment opportunities in computer-driven positions, such as programming or information systems analysis, has far outpaced the growth of physical jobs.

It's not just the working world that has experienced a reduction in physical activity. This reduction is happening in schools as well. Budget cuts and financial difficulties are forcing many schools to eliminate healthy programs like recess and physical education. When a school needs to cut back on expenses, it can't just cut the math program or the English program. Physical

education and recess are usually lower priorities. Falling test scores in many schools around the nation also have administrators looking for ways to increase classroom and study time. Again, gym classes and recess are the first to go. Interestingly, however, some new studies have shown that eliminating physical activity from the school day does not help students learn better or increase test scores; lack of physical activity may actually make students' academic performance worse.

Even when they're not in school or at work, many Americans are still not taking the opportunity to exercise. Of course, with busy, fast-paced lives, many people may feel that they are never anywhere but at school or work. This is not the case. Americans today actually have more leisure time than ever before, but most are not using it to enjoy active hobbies. In general, activities such as biking that were extremely popular in the past are not nearly as prevalent as they once were. An increase in the amount of time people spend watching television or on the computer may be the top contributors to this reduction in physical leisure activities.

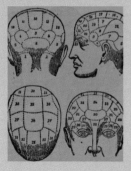

Behavior: An Environmental Factor?

A common quote says that "Children learn what they live." In other words, we learn most of our behaviors from our parents. Most of us have seen pictures of a little girl putting on makeup while her mother does the same thing in the background or of a little boy pretending to shave while his father does so. Watching a parent is the basis for most of our behaviors and tendencies. Not surprisingly, eating and activity habits are learned in the same way that other behaviors are learned.

Some people would argue that behavior, because it is learned from our surroundings, is an environmental factor. Most behaviors have roots in the home and are modified by the behaviors of other people over time. For example, children are first raised in the home environment and adopt the behaviors of that home. Then the children go to school. In the school environment, they mix with children who have different behaviors formed from different home environments. In this new environment, the children may influence each other, and some behaviors may blend. Other environmental factors could also influence one's behavior. For example, if one suddenly falls on hard economic times, she may have to cut back on some of her favorite activities to save money. If a person suddenly experiences a surge in wealth, she may take up more expensive pleasures than she previously engaged in.

It is not difficult to see how behavior can seem to be environmental. Children learn to eat as their parents eat, and children learn to enjoy physical activity when they are exposed to it at a young age. When parents do not encourage physical play, replacing a ball with a game console for example, a child may never develop an appreciation for playing outside. Despite the obviously environmental influences on behavior, however, behavior itself is not a true environmental factor. Behavior is about making choices, even though sometimes they may be very difficult to make. Behavior is internal. It is part of our personalities. Therefore, having a parent admonish you for not cleaning your plate, for example, would be an environmental factor on your eating habits, but your actual behavior of cleaning your plate is a choice; you could have chosen to resist the environmental influence and not clean your plate.

To be truthful, behavior, even though it is not an environmental factor, does play a large role in obesity. People who choose to always clean their plates, no matter how much food is on them, put themselves at greater risk for energy imbalance simply because of the amount of food they are ingesting. A choice can be made to stop eating and save that food for another meal. We also exercise choice when ordering food at restaurants. Ordering the next larger size of french fries with a fast-food meal adds hundreds of calories to the meal. Similarly, upsizing a drink can double the amount of empty calo-

ries taken in. The energy balance is thrown off by choices like this. We are programmed by our environment to think more is better, and our behavior reflects this programming. More, of course, is not always better, and you have a choice to control your behavior to reflect what you know. A certain number of Calories are required to maintain a healthy body weight, and it is easier than ever to eat more than is needed. One or two bad choices a day, if made consistently over time, can lead to obesity.

Simply making good choices is not always that easy. As we've seen, genetics cause some people to have difficulty controlling their hunger. If your body thinks you need more food, it is very hard to tell it "no." The feeling of endless hunger can be a strong driving force to keep the food coming. Furthermore, if you are unaware of how environmental factors have influenced your behavior and how that behavior is influencing your health, you will find it very difficult to make better choices. Understanding why we make the choices we make is a key part of making better choices in the future.

Genetics may play a significant role in a person's susceptibility to obesity, but as we've just seen, environmental factors are also contributing to the epidemic. Unfortunately, these environmental factors are occurring on both sides of the energy-balance equation. Americans are consuming more energy on the one hand and decreasing physical activity on the other. A recent study called *Coronary Artery Disease in Young Adults* (CARDIA) tracked hundreds of individuals for a span of many years and found that only about 25 percent were able to resist gaining weight over the course of the study. Americans' energy balance has clearly been tipped in favor of gaining weight.

Chapter 5

The Effect of Socioeconomic Status

- Access to Affordable Health Care

- Obesity, Socioeconomic Status, and Education

- Socioeconomic Status and Diet

- Low Socioeconomic Status and Low Activity Rates

Another environmental influence on people's health (and one that most people have little control over) is socioeconomic status. Several studies have shown that socioeconomic status and health are linked. Socioeconomic status is the place or level a person occupies in society based on resources like one's wealth, education, and employment. People with lots of wealth, for example, have a high socioeconomic status, while people with little money have a low socioeconomic status. Typically, having a low socioeconomic status puts people at increased risk of developing certain dangerous health conditions like heart disease. People with a high socioeconomic status suffer from various serious illnesses (and from illness in general) less often than people of lower status.

Why would the amount of money and other resources a person has make a person more or less likely to develop a disease? Why should wealthier people also get to be healthier than poorer people? The situation sounds a bit like a cruel cosmic joke. Once you begin examining the issues, however, it's easy to see how being of a lower socioeconomic status could increase the risks to your health.

Access to Affordable Health Care

Perhaps the biggest reason people of lower socioeconomic status are at greater health risk is that (at least in the United States) the less money you have, the less access you have to high-quality health care. Health care is extremely expensive. In many areas of the country, even a routine doctor's visit can cost more than fifty dollars. Just a few blood tests can cost hundreds of dollars. One trip to the emergency room can cost thousands of dollars. Few people in the United States can afford to pay for regular routine medical care let alone for a big hospital bill on their own.

The *prohibitive* cost of medical care is why people have health insurance. Health insurance works by guaranteeing that if a person should ever get really sick or badly injured, there will be someone (in this case the health insurance company) to cover the bills. When people have health insurance, they (or sometimes their employers) pay a certain amount of money every month to the health insurance company. In exchange, the health insurance company pays all or most of the person's medical expenses. If the person never gets sick or needs medical care, then the health insurance company has made a profit. If the person does become seriously ill and need lots of care, the insurance company has to pay. Unfortunately, like health care itself, health insurance is extremely expensive, so expensive that most people of low socioeconomic status can't afford it.

If you don't have health insurance, you are less likely to go see a doctor, even if you really need to. This puts people of lower socioeconomic status at greater risk both for developing health problems and for experiencing more severe consequences from those health problems than they would experience if they had greater access to medical care.

Clearly, a person who never saw a doctor would be at an increased risk for developing some health conditions, especially those that can be prevented or that can be easily cured if detected early. But what does this have to do with obesity? Many health professionals feel that individuals of lower socioeconomic status have a greater risk of developing obesity. Doctors and researchers disagree greatly about whether obesity and social class are tied and, if so, how they are related. Some studies have come to the conclusion that there is no relationship. Other researchers believe that obesity causes a person to be poor (because people with obesity face far more discrimination in education and hiring than people of lower weight), rather than being poor causing obesity. However, large numbers of researchers and doctors believe that poor people are far more likely to be obese for a variety of reasons.

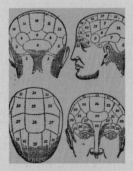

Obesity, Socioeconomic Status, and Education

One way that obesity and socioeconomic status may be linked is through education. Educational level varies greatly with socioeconomic status. Basically, people with less money usually have less education than people with more money. There are two reasons for this. First, although public education in the United States is free through the twelfth grade, higher education is expensive. Public schools in poorer neighborhoods also have less funding than schools in wealthier areas or private schools. Underfunded schools cannot afford the same teachers, books, and equipment and therefore often can't provide the same quality of education provided by other schools. In many cases, the less money you have, the less and lower-quality education you can afford. The second reason people of lower socioeconomic status tend to have less education is because high-paying jobs tend to require a high level of education. People of low socioeconomic status, therefore, are stuck in a vicious cycle: they don't have enough money to afford the education, and they can't get the money they need because the better jobs require the higher education they can't afford.

It is apparent that education strongly influences health. People with more education tend to be better informed about health risks, ways to prevent health problems, and what the body requires to maintain good health. Take smoking, for example. Years ago it seemed like everybody smoked. Few people knew the full health risks of smoking. As these risks became known, however, people began to give up smoking. The more educated a person was concerning the impact smoking could have on his health, the more likely he was to give up the habit. Huge public education campaigns began to inform people about the risks of smoking, and schools became the major battlefront on the war against cigarettes. Today, fewer and fewer people smoke, and the decrease in smoking rates is directly linked to an increase in education.

People with more education tend to be better informed about health risks, ways to prevent health problems, and what the body requires to maintain good health.

Because these education campaigns were public in nature, they reached people of both high and low socioeconomic status, and smoking has been reduced across the board (although smoking rates are still higher among people of low socioeconomic status with less education than among people of high socioeconomic status with more education).

Public education campaigns about obesity and its health risks, however, are still in their infancy. Today, people with the most education tend to be best informed about obesity and its prevention. The less education a person has, the fewer resources he has to help him recognize, understand, and cope with the factors that cause obesity.

Socioeconomic Status and Diet

Socioeconomic status also affects diet. Eating a balanced diet that is high in vegetables, fruits, and whole grains and low in simple carbohydrates and unhealthy fats is an essential part of maintaining a healthy weight. Many people of low socioeconomic status have difficulty affording a balanced diet. Inexpensive foods are often very low in true nutrition and high in salt, sugar, and fat. Therefore, low-cost diets that are high in fat and sugar are typical in many low-income families.

The less education a person has, the fewer resources he has to help him recognize, understand, and cope with the factors that cause obesity.

As one example, consider the cost of a value meal at a fast-food restaurant compared to a grilled fish fillet, baked potato, and salad at a sit-down restaurant. Chances are your healthier sit-down restaurant meal costs many times that of the unhealthy fast-food meal. If a person with little money can afford to go to a restaurant at all, it is more likely to be an inexpensive fast-food restaurant than a restaurant serving healthier fare.

The problem of healthy food's affordability, however, isn't just in restaurants. It's in grocery stores as well. Lean meats, like fish and skinless chicken breasts, cost far more than high-fat ground beef and frozen pizzas. A bag of potato chips is much cheaper than most fresh fruits and vegetables. Healthy, balanced meals can be more expensive (and also more time consuming to prepare) than unhealthy, nutritionally imbalanced meals. The fact that unhealthy foods are often less expensive than healthier foods is thought to be an important factor in why people of lower socioeconomic status may be at higher risk for obesity. The fact that unhealthy meals, like a hamburger served with potato chips, are much quicker and easier to prepare than healthy meals, like freshly made salad, steamed vegetables, grilled fish, and brown rice, is another factor that may influence people of low socioeconomic status to have unhealthy diets. After all, if you are a single parent working to support a family, or if you are working two jobs to keep up with bills, you probably have little time or energy left for cooking.

According to the American Dietetic Association (ADA), one key to a healthy diet is to moderate, not eliminate, favorite foods because eliminating foods is rarely successful long term. In fact, the ADA says that all foods can fit into a healthy diet—what's most important is eating a balanced diet over time, rather than any one food or meal.

Low Socioeconomic Status and Low Activity Rates

There is also ample evidence that people of lower socioeconomic status have lower physical activity rates than people of high socioeconomic status. Some of the reasons are easy to see. For example, many Americans today get their exercise at fitness clubs, but these clubs, while offering many useful (and often fun) services, are very expensive. They are certainly out of the price range of many Americans.

Less obvious, but perhaps just as important, is the fact that people of low socioeconomic status tend to live in less pleasant areas of cities, areas that often have higher crime rates than wealthier areas. Many of these areas are not safe or appealing for casual walking, and parks tend to be poorly maintained if they exist at all. If you can't safely go outside to take a walk or play a game of basketball, it can be very difficult to get that daily hour of physical activity you need to stay healthy.

Another reason people of lower socioeconomic status have lower physical activity rates may actually be emotional. Let's face it. It's not always easy to exercise. In fact, after a difficult day at work or school, exercise may be the very last thing you want to do. For people of low socioeconomic status, motivation may be even harder to come by. Because their life circumstances can be very difficult (it may be a struggle to just get food on the table), people with less money and resources tend to have higher rates of depression, something that can certainly reduce one's desire to exercise. And of course, as with cooking, time is another factor that can discourage people from exercising. If you are working two jobs and barely have time to cook, where are you going to find the time to exercise?

A study completed in 2003 by the Medical College of Georgia indicates a relationship between socioeconomic status and genetics in determining obesity. The researchers came to the conclusion that people of all social classes carried the "bad gene" that they were studying. This bad gene was present both in people who were and were not obese. When the researchers looked at social class and obesity together, however, they discovered that poor people with the gene were obese far more often than well-to-do people with the gene. They interpreted this to mean that socioeconomic status had a significant role in controlling whether the effects of the gene showed or not.

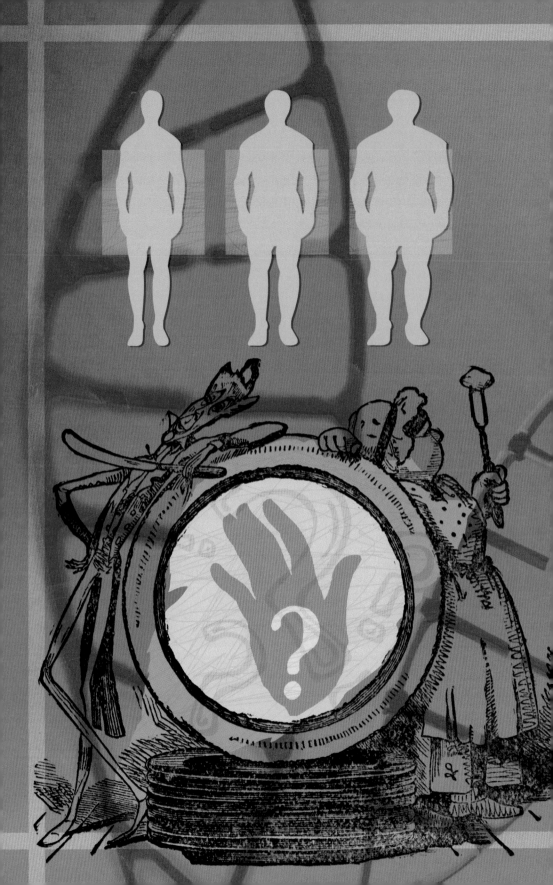

Chapter 6

It's a Simple Question of Nature vs. Nurture, Right?

The Great Debate

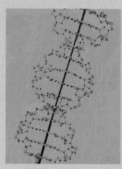

Understanding that there are both genetic and environmental factors influencing rising obesity rates leaves us with a question: Is obesity caused more by "nature" or more by "nurture"? In the scientific community there are few debates as heated as nature vs. nurture. The nature side of the argument says that genetics is the most important factor in determining how a person will look and act, how healthy she will be, even how successful she will be in life. The nurture side contends that it is the environment a person is brought up in that will determine most of the important aspects of her life. It is nice sometimes to have a clear winner in a debate. That will not happen in this case. In truth, it is almost impossible to separate the effects of nature from the effects of nurture when it comes to certain things. Most of the time, it is probably better to think of each as having some affect on the outcome.

Genetics gets the clear nod when it comes to determining things like eye color, hair color, or height. Many traits are clearly controlled by our genes and are not affected by the environment (unless some extremely strong environmental factor, like exposure to a serious toxin, for example, alters the genetic code and changes the course of one's development). Genetics can also be used to determine if a person will be at risk of developing a problem later in life. Some people have a parent (or parents) who died early as a result of heart disease. In this case, genetics can provide an early warning for the individual, who can then take steps to prevent suffering a similar fate. Genetics can often provide us with enough information to take steps to prevent or at least reduce one's chances of developing many deadly diseases.

Unfortunately, obesity is not a case where we can rely specifically on genetics to determine our risk. It is true that in studies of identical twins living together doctors have reported that both children usually have the same body type and approximately the same BMI. Several studies of adopted chil-

Many traits are clearly controlled by our genes and are not affected by the environment (unless some extremely strong environmental factor, like exposure to a serious toxin, for example, alters the genetic code and changes the course of one's development).

dren have shown that the children are more like their birth parents than their adoptive parents in terms of body type and BMI. Results like these would lead us to believe that nature is governing our weight and body size. Not necessarily. It is clear that there is some genetic component to obesity, but no one knows how powerful the effect is. With so many environmental factors also contributing to rising obesity rates, it could be the environment more than one's genetic code leading to weight issues. If a person with a genetic predisposition for obesity was never exposed to environmental factors that encouraged energy imbalance, perhaps that genetic predisposition would never be triggered and the obesity would never actually materialize.

Genetic risk factors are inherited from one's parents. Doctors often report that obese people have obese children, so the natural thought process is that the children were genetically predisposed to obesity. But some aspects of one's environment are also inherited, and behavior is also learned from one's parents. So while obesity may run in families, the causes can be environmental and behavioral rather than simply genetic. In other words, the parents have a problem controlling their weight for a variety of reasons, and the children "inherit" the tendencies of their parents. Bad eating habits and lack of physical activity are trends that can be set in a family because children tend to learn what they live. The home environment can have a huge effect on the health of a child. The children of obese individuals may find themselves at risk simply because of the habits of their parents. Children of people who smoke are far more likely to become smokers themselves than the children from nonsmoking homes. The same can likely be said of children whose parents are obese.

> *Genetic risk factors are inherited from one's parents.*

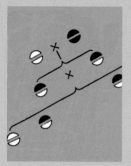

Do You Think You Can Assess Your Own Risk?

Obesity tends to run in families, as we have previously discussed. The causes of obesity are varied, so it is often very difficult to accurately determine who is at risk. Family history does however tend to be accurate for assessing risk in the case of obesity for various reasons.

A family history that extends back three generations can provide valuable information for determining whether an individual has an increased risk of developing obesity. Perhaps the best way to build a family history is to create a *pedigree chart*. Below is a sample pedigree that shows the existence of a disease within a family over several generations.

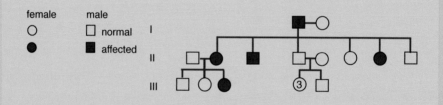

Using the information contained in a pedigree chart, genetic counselors can determine whether it is necessary to perform more detailed screening tests. DNA screening is a procedure that looks for the presence of certain genes in the person's genetic makeup. DNA screening can be used when the evidence suggests that there is reason for more information. Just a small

One hour of walking at a moderate pace (20 min/mile) uses about the same amount of energy that is in one jelly-filled doughnut (300 Calories).

sample of blood is all that is required to gather a large amount of information. Most often, the blood test is sent to a laboratory for examination. Special techniques allow scientists to determine if the blood contains certain genes, thereby providing an idea of whether the patient is at risk for disorders that are genetic in nature. Construct a pedigree of your family for the last two generations using the one on page 92 as a guide. Shade in the box or circle of any family member who was overweight. Based on you pedigree, do you think that there is an increased risk of obesity in your family?

A pedigree chart and awareness of a person's genetics alone, however, cannot tell an individual how great his risk is of developing obesity. Other factors also must be considered. Another critical factor in assessing risk is behavior. The person will be asked to answer a list of questions about their personal habits. Sometimes this exposes some tough realities; other times it shows that the problem is not something the person has any control over. Learning about personal behavior can be the step that separates the people who are genuinely in need of medical help from those who are not.

> *You would have to run for two and a half hours at ten minutes per mile to burn the Calories you would get from a fast food "meal" containing a double cheeseburger, extra-large fries, and a 24 oz. soft drink (1,500 Calories).*
>
> *(The Surgeon General's Call to Action to Prevent and Decrease Obesity and Overweight, 2001)*

Now that you have a basic understanding of the methods used to assess risk you can try it. Simply answer the questions below as accurately as you can.

- Do you take less than twenty minutes to eat your average meal?
- After finishing your meal, do you still feel hungry?
- When you sit down to eat, do you eat everything put in front of you regardless of the portion size?
- Do you fail to exercise at a moderate level at least three days each week?
- Do you fail to eat a balanced diet each and every day?
- Does your diet include large amounts of high-sugar or high-fat foods?

If you answered yes to two or more of these questions, you may be at risk of becoming overweight. The best way to prevent weight gain is to control the factors that are known to lead to it. Genetics may or may not play a role even if your pedigree shows a long history of obesity because it is very difficult to tell whether the problem is actually caused by genetic factors. Families tend to pass down more than just genes. Eating and exercise habits are learned from daily life.

One small chocolate chip cookie has approximately 50 Calories. You burn approximately 50 Calories by walking briskly for 10 minutes. The difference between a large gourmet chocolate chip cookie (200 Calories) and a small chocolate chip cookie could be accounted for by about 40 minutes of raking leaves (an activity that would burn 200 Calories).

> *One thing is clear. Even if a person is genetically predisposed to obesity, he is not doomed to a lifetime of struggling with obesity.*

Most of the time genetics can indicate that a person is predisposed to a certain health problem but cannot actually predict that the problem will develop. People who know that there is a risk of heart disease, for instance, will take steps to make sure they do not have heart problems. In other words, they will change their behaviors to avoid a serious health problem. Nature collides with nurture, and the problem can be avoided.

One thing is clear. Even if a person is genetically predisposed to obesity, he is not doomed to a lifetime of struggling with obesity. Many factors come into play in the determination of body shape, and genetics may have an effect, but that does not by any means guarantee the outcome. Personal choices and environment are very important in controlling obesity as well. In other words, there is some aspect of each in the development of obesity, and no one factor seems to have a greater effect than the others. Whether the factors contributing to a person's excess weight are genetic, environmental, behavioral, or a combination, being educated about the causes and health risks of obesity is the first step toward managing the crisis in our own lives and in society as a whole.

Glossary

AIDS: acquired immunodeficiency syndrome—a condition characterized by the destruction of the immune system and caused by the human immunodeficiency virus (HIV).

chronic: To be long lasting or to recur frequently.

coronary heart disease: A condition characterized by hardening of the arteries to the heart, which can result in diminished blood flow, heart attack, and death.

genetics: The study of how traits are passed on through generations.

gluttony: The act of eating or drinking excessively.

mechanization: The process of replacing human workers with machines.

monastery: A dwelling for a religious community.

monk: A male religious devotee living apart from the nonreligious community and dedicating himself to prayer, contemplation, and work.

osteoarthritis: A condition of the joints in which the cartilage breaks down resulting in pain, stiffness, and decreased mobility.

pedigree chart: A chart showing the direct relatives of a person.

predisposition: A susceptibility, based on hereditary or other factors, to develop a disease.

prohibitive: To be too expensive or otherwise unattainable for someone to get.

rudimentary: The basic level.

sedentary: To spend most of the time seated; not requiring much movement.

selective breeding: Intentionally pairing certain individuals for reproduction for the purposes of manipulating the characteristics of the next generation.

sociologists: People who study the institutions and development of human society.

stigmatization: The process of being labeled socially unacceptable.

susceptibility: The likelihood of being affected by something.

type 2 diabetes: A disease characterized by the body's inability to correctly use insulin.

Further Reading

Behan, Eileen. *Fit Kids: Raising Physically and Emotionally Strong Kids with Real Food*. New York: Pocket Publishing, 2001.

Brownell, Kelly D. and Katherine Battle Horgen. *Food Fight: The Inside Story of the Food Industry, America's Obesity Crisis, and What We Can Do About It.* Chicago: McGraw-Hill, 2003.

Clark, William R. and Michael Grunstein. *Are We Hardwired? The Role of Genes in Human Behavior*. New York: Oxford University Press, 2000.

Critser, Greg. *Fat Land: How Americans Became the Fattest People in the World*. Boston: Mariner Books, 2004.

Gallagher, Winifred. *Just the Way You Are: How Heredity and Experience Create the Individual*. New York: Random House, 1997.

Hamer, Dean H. and Peter Copeland. *Living with Our Genes: Why They Matter More Than You Think*. New York: Doubleday, 1999.

Johnson, Susan and Laurel Mellin. *Just for Kids! (Obesity Prevention Workbook)*. San Anselmo, Calif.: Balboa Publishing, 2002.

Levenstein, Harvey. *Paradox of Plenty: A Social History of Eating in Modern America, Revised Edition*. Berkeley: University of California Press, 2003.

Medina, John J. *The Genetic Inferno: Inside the Seven Deadly Sins*. Cambridge, U.K.: Cambridge University Press, 2000.

Pierce, Benjamin A. *The Family Genetic Sourcebook*. New York: J. Wiley, 1990.

Pool, Robert. *Fat: Fighting the Obesity Epidemic*. New York: Oxford University Press, 2001.

Rimm, Sylvia and Eric Rimm. *Rescuing the Emotional Lives of Our Overweight Children: What Our Kids go Through and How We Can Help Them*. Emmaus, Pa.: Rodale Books, 2004.

Shell, Ellen Ruppel. *The Hungry Gene: The Science of Fat and the Future of Thin*. New York: Atlantic Monthly Press, 2002.

Wann, Marilyn. *Fat! So? Because You Don't Have to Apologize for Your Size*. Berkeley. Calif.: Ten Speed Press, 1999.

For More Information

About Our Kids: Obesity and Overweight
www.aboutourkids.org/aboutour/articles/gr_obesity_03.html

Aim for a Healthy Weight: Assess Your Risk
www.nhlbi.nih.gov/health/public/heart/obesity/lose_wt/risk.htm#limitations

American Obesity Association
www.obesity.org

Definition and Classification of Obesity
www.endotext.org/obesity/obesity1/obesityframe1.htm

Environmental Contributions to Obesity
www.endotext.org/obesity/obesity7/obesity7.htm

Genomics and Obesity
www.cdc.gov/genomics/info/perspectives/files/obesedit.htm

The Learning Center
www.hebs.scot.nhs.uk/learningcentre/obesity/intro/index.cfm

Obesity: Causes
www.weight-loss-i.com/obesity-causes.htm

Obesity and Environment Factsheet
www.niehs.nih.gov/oc/factsheets/obesity.htm

Statistics Related to Overweight and Obesity
win.niddk.nih.gov/statistics/index.htm

Your Child: Obesity and Overweight
www.med.umich.edu/1libr/yourchild/obesity.htm

Publisher's note:
The Web sites listed on these pages were active at the time of publication. The publisher is not responsible for Web sites that have changed their addresses or discontinued operation since the date of publication. The publisher will review the Web sites and update the list upon each reprint.

Index

Picture Credits

Biographies

William Hunter lives in western New York with his wife, Miranda. Bill graduated from Fredonia University with a B.S. in biology and the University at Buffalo with an M.A. in biology. Bill and his wife have written several other nonfiction books for young adults, including *Staying Safe: A Teen's Guide to Sexually Transmitted Diseases.*

Dr. Victor F. Garcia is the co-director of the Comprehensive Weight Management Center at Cincinnati Children's Hospital Medical Center. He is a board member of Discover Health of Greater Cincinnati, a fellow of the American College of Surgeons, and a two-time winner of the Martin Luther King Humanitarian Award.